Handwriting Practice Pap[illegible]

MW00464257

100 Blank Pages of Kindergarten Writing Paper with Wide Lines

This book belongs to:

Made in the USA
Middletown, DE
13 November 2022

14794836R00057